To My Wife & The Cats

And to all my past, present & future Guests

Customer Service Theory

Customer Service Theory by Jeremy Zuber

© 2017 by Jeremy Zuber. All rights reserved.

No part of this book may be reproduced in any written, electronic, recording, or photocopying form without written permission of the author, Jeremy Zuber.

Books may be purchased in quantity and/or special sales by contacting the author, Jeremy Zuber at
ServiceTheory@gmail.com

Published by: Amazon CreateSpace
First Edition

Contents

Preface 5

The Sylvester Stallone Theory 8

Need Based Service: Creating service avenues through high probability needs 15

Riddle Me This: Passive vs. Aggressive Service 20

The Cat Sweater Theory: How to make instant connections 25

The Chameleon Mentality: Adapting to unchanging circumstances 29

Layered Service: Creating experiences worth remembering 35

Lost in Translation: Speaking the right service language 39

Gone Fishin': Reeling in Big Angry Fish 46

3D Service: The Ultimate Experience 62

Theories in Action: 69

Guest Letters 83

Closing 87

Preface

Over a decade ago, as a bellman at a Four Diamond property in the stunning northwest corner of Wyoming. Part of my significant daily checklist was to deliver ice to all thirty seven quaintly appointed cabins on the multi acre landscape. A recently retired couple checked in and it was discovered that they were visiting for a fiftieth wedding anniversary on the following day. I had an idea. This was the first time an idea such as this had boarded all passengers on my train of thought and the locomotive had gathered a full head of steam. I made sure to get an early start on the 6am shift, so there would be time to craft a little surprise. Utilizing the fifty percent employee discount, I selected a lovely little card from the gift shop and penned a little poem for them. To this day, I regret not making a copy of it, but in the excitement of the moment I failed to think of the scrapbook that would one day be assembled on my living room floor. I parked my ice cart at their door and knocked. No answer. Surely they must be on the excursion to Yellowstone that they had planned, so the opportunity was at hand! I filled their ice bucket and placed the card next to their wine glasses, as they had mentioned they had a special wine selected for that evening. The rest of the day was a blur, and I simply could not wait until they read their card. I was off at three, so I figured they had yet to return to their lovely, albeit temporary, abode. I went for my afternoon run around String Lake, a lovely yet difficult three mile circuit featuring some challenging hills with spectacular views from above. As I rounded the final bend that took me back to my own cabin, I saw the happy couple sipping their special vintage on their patio. They recognized me and waved vigorously for me to come by. They both shrugged off the age that surely plagued their joints after their lengthy adventure and while I was expecting a nice conversation, I was met by tearful hugs with the Mrs. clutching the card that was written for them. The outpouring of love extended that day between near strangers taught me one of the most valuable lessons in guest service that a person could ever learn. That incredible moment captured my heart, and I have pursued the art of hospitality ever since. There is an old saying that elegant service means to be friendly but not familiar, yet there are moments when a person can tip-toe that line and reach into someone's heart and life to resonate in the most powerful way. Through my entirely accidental voyage via various posts in hospitality, I have found that there are indeed theories of guest service – theories that can be bent and manipulated to the brink of becoming law. A theory by definition is: a belief, policy, or procedure proposed or followed as the basis of action. Essentially, the ideas and methods discussed are based upon desired results that occur by following the presented ideas and methods. However, circumstances could potentially arise in which the theory breaks down, but when properly interpreted and utilized these principles have granted much success in the way of winning the hearts and minds of my guests, clients, and fellow colleagues. Welcome to a journey through the world of service theory and I wish you much success along the way!

The Sylvester Stallone Theory

Conceived many years ago and the first of all my service principles, this has encouraged me to go beyond ordinary in the face of unexpected requests and challenging situations. Let us begin. Sylvester Stallone is easily my favorite actor of all time. Sure there were some Hollywood busts along the way (i.e. the mid nineties catalog), but at the end of the day he IS Rocky Balboa. Not many people can say they went toe to toe with Ivan Drago, right? Thus begins the origin of this theory. I was twenty three and working as a Concierge on the island of St. John in the sunny Caribbean. It was January and we were at the apex of "the high season". There were parties, late nights and plenty of ways for me and my band of idiotic friends to watch a bleary eyed sunrise lazily wake up the town of Cruz Bay. On one particular night we had concocted major plans. My buddy was house sitting a four bedroom condominium and the festivities were already under way. Plans had been in the works for weeks the whole gang was ready to go. It was going to be fantastic! My only problem was that I was working until ten, while most of my buddies had secured the night off. How typical. It was difficult to focus on the tasks of the day, but somehow I clambered from one guest booking to another as the clock bludgeoned its way towards closing time. I essentially ran the desk at night with most managers and supervisors having gone home for the day. However, always playing by the book the desk stayed open until the clock struck zero, or in this case 10:00pm. Fortunately, the buzz of the dinner hour was but hush with only one couple sipping dirty martinis in the lobby, so I was simply wrapping up the details for the next day's morning shift. At half past nine, I was in chill mode and counting down. The clock began to crawl like a baby on a blanket and my phone was vibrating like it was New Year's Eve. My cerebral rocket pack was on and I was ready to jet! It was 9:58pm, and right when I truly believed that I was in the clear, out of nowhere a lady appeared who was clearly quite far along with a bun in the oven. It was practically a loaf.

Wanting to bolt up the stairs, I balked for a just second too long. She wobbled up to the desk doing the type of side to side shuffle that is the number one dance move for soon-to-be mothers, and she requested, of all things, a hot fudge sundae. "A hot fudge sundae at this hour!!??" said an unruly voice in the back of my head. I was less than thrilled about this prospect. She began to explain. Apparently, she fell asleep early after her prenatal massage and missed the dinner hour. Since all restaurants had closed at 9:30pm, she was now in dire need of sustenance. Now at that moment, I had every right to offer an apology and let her know that all outlets were unfortunately closed. After all, I was only the concierge, I didn't have a proper health card, and it wasn't my fault. What did I owe this random person accosting my desk asking for something so outlandish at that hour? Surely, I was being inconvenienced! However, something occurred to me at the very moment. It was as if time stood still and I asked myself; "What if this was Sylvester Stallone?" What would I say? How would I respond? My logical conclusion at that point was that I would say "Absolutely Mr. Stallone! One hot fudge sundae coming right up!", and then I would disappear and work as much ice creamy magic as one could muster and craft the finest, gourmet hot fudge sundae he had ever enjoyed. I suddenly felt ashamed at my reluctance. If I would be so willing to do that for Sly, a regular paying guest at my resort, why would I have so much hesitation, if not disgust, when somebody else approached with that same request? It was then that I made my choice. I didn't bother to tell the guest that all of our restaurants are closed, but I could still do it – just so she would know I am going out of my way. That is a really lame thing that some customer service people do, by the way. If you can do it, do it and don't go into detail. I also didn't bother to tell her that I would have to go all the way up to security to get the key for the freezer and then come back, so she would have to wait awhile (people also do this to try to make the customer say to not bother with it and then thank them for trying). I only told her what she needed to know. One, I could do it. Two, it will be ready in a flash. Three, I will personally serve it to her. **Quick Service Tip**: Making powerful verbal contracts and following and personally following through is the quickest way to earn trust. After I had gathered her name and room number, I said "You can have a seat right here in the breezeway, and I will be right back with your hot fudge sundae." You can imagine the shock on her face when I said it so matter-of-factly. Off I went with no thoughts about parties or friends but rather simply focused on making this sundae *happen*. I collected the key from Security, which under normal circumstances would have garnered me the evil eye, but that fact was that our nighttime security guards were on two missions per night - get as much sleep and do the least amount of work possible. After getting zero interrogation, I now had the ice cream making magic in the palm of my hand. With the aforementioned magic, I proceeded to create the most grandiose sundae possible, skipping no steps and I even gave her small bowls with condiments, so she could make it exactly to her liking. We had a ball talking about everything under the sun that evening. Despite all the amazing experiences she had around the island, she said that the ice cream was the most unforgettable moment of her stay and her only wish was that she could find service like that in her other travels around the world. What is the lesson here? Service bias is a very dangerous thing.

One cannot simply pick and choose when to deliver the goods. Serve or do not serve. As hosts to our customers we must treat them all alike whether or not they are recognizable. Our guests and customers choose us - we don't choose them. We market and sell ourselves to them through various channels and we must accept ALL the results, not just the easy ones or the ones that we choose to like. If a customer asks for something unconventional, we have a choice whether or not to provide it for them - and such as life, we must live with the consequences of the choices we make. In order to simplify things, I apply the Sylvester Stallone Theory every single day. Sometimes a guest requests a gazillion pillows or a bunch of extra bottles of shampoo. One time someone called to ask if I could assist with putting the cremated remains of a relative into the ocean for them, since they couldn't make the trip. Boy, was that an odd package to receive during the holidays, but I did it anyway. That said, sometimes even I feel like hesitating because a request seems ridiculous or kind of a stretch, but when I apply the Sylvester Stallone Theory, it helps me make the right choice for the right reason. Serve all or serve none, and the beauty is that the choice is yours.

Summary: *Don't lose focus on your goal of 100% excellence in guest service – 100% of the time. It is not our job to validate requests or selectively serve our guests or even our colleagues based on how we feel at the moment. When you resist the urge to selectively serve people, you will find that you maximize your positive results every time.*

Need Based Service: Creating service avenues through high probability needs

Nobody loves a salesperson. In fact, people are motivated by need more than desire, although modern day commercials attempt to blur the lines between the two. One of the keys to winning people is discovering what their immediate needs are. Psychologist Abraham Maslow tapped into this idea with his theory of human motivation. Instead of studying the ill prototypes of humankind, he studied the finest one percent of collegiate minds. In doing so, he was able to define and categorize the levels of need for humankind. The final outcome was a pyramid that encompasses the concepts that we feel make us real and definite "people". There are five levels to the pyramid, and starting from the foundation to the precipice it is as follows: Physiological, Safety, Love/Belonging, Esteem, and Self Actualization. In luxury hospitality, we must be honest with ourselves and understand that we reside in between Esteem and Self Actualization. We are not a primary need – our customer base is different than that of your average roadside motel. People MUST have a roof over their head. They also must drink water. People don't **need** marble bathtubs or the finest diamond purified, reverse osmosis sparkling beverage. However, once you enter into the ranks of luxury hospitality, people no longer operate on need but rather by choice, customization, and access. We are in a business where image is everything, and we have guests who want to be seen and actualized as the image that we portray via our marketing and advertising. For our survival we must understand what we are and where we fit in from a "human" perspective. However, in making guests "feel" a certain way in order to make them become what they wish to be, it starts at the very base of the pyramid. We focus much energy on the fiscal bottom line: up-sells, cross-sells, ADR (average daily rate) and occupancy. However, it is by tapping into the nerve that is need based, that we will drive those results. You can practically throw financials out the window because without the need for people to feel a certain way, there is no ADR. After all, remember that we are sitting near the top of the pyramid. In delivering service, one of the most important things to do right away is to uncover the most basic physiological needs of our guests. Why do you think that reception areas feature some type of arrival snack or drink in their advertising? One hotel company bases an entire advertising campaign on a cookie upon arrival at the front desk for Pete's sake! Talk about dangling the proverbial carrot. The reason for this is that they are attempting to address the basic need for food as a reason to visit that particular hotel and feel "at home". This makes the customer say "Geez, if they meet my most basic need when I arrive, they must be able to fulfill my other needs", thus increasing the likelihood of booking through one channel or another. With that understanding, it is now important to train our staff to get after those needs the moment a guest strolls through the revolving door. One discovery early on in my career is that I could educate my guests, and once they viewed me as a source for sustenance and survival, they would continue to come back, often times specifically to wait for my individual services. It was less about the actual service I was providing and more about them feeling the increased capacity for their own survival by visiting my "watering hole". By simply asking if they had a meal recently, it would always capture their attention. Even if they had a recent meal, in their mind, they knew they would need one later. By teaching them that I could lead them to the best option – specifically for them based on details I had learned from our conversation - they would continue to seek my advice. Luxury hospitality is just that - a luxury. We are more than just a roof over someone's head. We are an image, a brand, and an icon. We are a stylistic expression of personality ready to be customized and wrapped around the guest like the gift they are. We are not needed - as defined by Maslow - so we must create demand based on the understanding of a guest's primary needs. Knowing we fit in between Esteem and Self Actualization, it is best to start at the bottom of the pyramid – the primary needs to live - in order to bring the guest to the precipice of Self Actualization. The greater capacity we have to make people feel a certain way will have a lasting impact on the amazing business that we conduct every day and every night.

Summary: *It is okay to ask questions to guests and they love it when they feel you are interested in them. By starting with their most basic needs, we can then begin to deliver a full and dynamic experience. Educating the customer that you are source of survival, fulfillment and enjoyment will lead to benefits for you and for the customer.*

Riddle Me This: Passive vs. Aggressive Service

 vs.

Passive service is incredibly tiresome. It is tedious, frustrating, and creates service overhead - more phone calls, longer wait times, etc. What is passive service? Passive service is waiting to be asked for help. It begins with body language, and rears its ugly face all over service based establishments. Employees force people to come to them. When was the last time someone came over to YOU to offer assistance? By the way, it doesn't count if they were trying to sell you something. Passive service makes the customer do the work. Then comes the verbiage. *"Can I get you anything else?" "Will that be all?" "Do you need help with your bags?"* See how that sounds? We make our guests feel like needy little pests! It is a nice way of saying "I can help you (would rather not) but you are going to have to ask for it". A more aggressive stance is to observe and then act, especially in a hotel. Would you rather be a robot with a simple input/output function or a multi-tasking service machine? Anytime I witness someone looking around, hesitating, or I hear them asking their friend a question about where they are going (yes, I am a voracious eavesdropper), I take action. People shouldn't be forced to lay down at the altar of those who can provide service and subsequently plead for it. I discovered this early on as a Bellman when I first started working in hospitality. My simple college brain informed me that the more bags I handled, the more tips I would make. Simple! However, people were often turning down my services. After all, they had a parking space right next to their lovely cabin, so why would they "need" my services. In pondering my rather penniless circumstance, I decided to change how I worded my offer. The question now became a statement: "Hi! My name is Jeremy, I will be assisting you with your bags today!" From that point forward I was carrying more bags and consequently, making more money. It became less about offering assistance and more about educating my guest that the service I was about to provide was simply how it worked in our establishment. If the person declined, they were polite and they would say "it's okay, I got it" and I would simply engage them in conversation. I saw that by rephrasing my question into a statement, I created a service opportunity wherein I could emotionally impact my guest. With that in mind, isn't that what hotels are about? As leaders in our businesses, aggressive service is a practice that is imperative to success. The more service we provide, the more our guests will interpret a higher level of care, and they will naturally pay for it. Even as a Bellman, I saw that I could provide as little or as much service as I wished - it was all about how my guest was educated about my position and duties. Now we shall note the value of a question. With the aggressive mindset and the goal of providing more service to increase the perception of value, questions become incredibly valuable. The goal is to ask questions until you reach the point of being able to provide a service that the guest did NOT request. For example, if a guest came to my desk and inquired about activities for the day, I would provide them with three distinct options. Once we decided on their destination for the day, instead of wishing them a wonderful time, I would follow with a query of my own. "Do you have plans for this evening?", for example. Most folks would not be thinking that far ahead and I would then be set up to create an evening of adventure for them. However, if they had plans, then I would make a simple recommendation for something to do after their dinner arrangement. It is all about discovering the guest and voluntarily adding to their stay. THAT creates value. Once again, it is a process of getting enough information to provide an intuitive act. There is a soda company that bases an entire advertising campaign on putting common first names on their bottles. Why is it so successful? It is based on two fundamental principles that people value: Personalization and the service *being unexpected.* I am no psychologist, so I can't explain why it makes synapses and emotions move in unison, but all I know is that it works. As a guest, if you were to ask for room keys, a dinner reservation or directions and you only receive what you asked for, then you would likely give the individual a C minus – the result was expected. The final 10% of the conversation has 90% of the impact. One more question, leads to one more service, and if you multiply that by the number of hotel employees you have, the gains in perceived value will be exponential. The only way to know what a guest needs is simply to ask and then act. Be aggressive.

Summary: *Find ways to open service avenues. Don't be a robot! Change "Do you need help with that?" into "I will assist with those items!" Turn "Want me to call a taxi?" into "I'm calling a taxi for you!" Take questions and turn them into positive statements. Lastly, ask one more question to allow yourself the freedom to create something special for your customer.*

The Cat Sweater Theory: How to make instant connections

All guests have an emotional code – some simple and some complex – but EVERYBODY, myself included, has a code. When that code is entered, a flashing red button that is approximately 4 inches in diameter appears on the guest's forehead, at least in my imagination anyway. The button, when activated, makes the guest incredibly happy and also builds a personal connection. The secret to making guests happy is to make them feel important and if there is any meaning to the business we conduct, it is to locate and strike that button whenever it shows up (kind of like Contra if you have ever played the 8-bit Nintendo game). Anyhow, a fun example of this came during my career as a Concierge at a world class Caribbean resort. A woman in her early seventies shuffled up to my desk on a breezy winter morning. Aside from her gray-blue beehive and her crimson lipstick, I noticed she had a crew neck sweater with a big picture of a cat playing with a ball of yarn. I suddenly realized that this lovely lady only had a 1 digit code. I didn't need to enter it. It really would not behoove me financially or have any real impact on my life whatsoever. However, the thought struck me that my personal benefit was of no consequence here. In this business, it is our job to press the button and press it often. You don't have access to it by just making new keys, making a dinner reservation, or by cleaning someone's room. It is about customization. It is about creating conversations that will interest your clientele and it is the quickest way to learn about people. Luxury hospitality is about options, no? After that thought passed, I chose to enter the code by saying – "Ma'am, do you like cats?" Now to most, the question would be almost rhetorical. Of course she likes cats; she has a calico batting a giant red ball of yarn on her sweater! However, because of the customer/employee relationship, that phrase is fundamentally unnecessary, unexpected, and quite frankly, perfect. She wasn't frowning when she approached me, but she wasn't exactly smiling. The moment I made that simple inquiry, her soft, wrinkly eyes widened and she smiled as if I was giving her something that she had always treasured. She said to me "Oh my goodness, I love cats!" I had accessed and effectively pressed the button. It was so incredible that I decided to press it again, almost as if with each press candy would tumble from the sky. I said "tell me about your cats!" We then proceeded to have a delightful conversation, so delightful that she completely forgot what she came to ask for and had to return to the desk a few minutes later! From that point forward, I realized our true mission. Now some guests have codes that even the most advanced hacker would struggle with – capital letters, symbols, and strange characters. However, with the right technique and strategy, the codes can always be found (or at least 99.9% of the time, they can be found 99.9% of the time). I frequently coach team members that the reason we do this is because while these personal bonds we create may become strained due to service and product pitfalls, but they typically will not be broken. Only when the bonds fail to exist do we lose our guests and customers. People are surprisingly forgiving when it comes to faulty product, but they tend to reserve no forgiveness for faulty people.

Summary: *Find ways to bond with your customer. Many view this as pointless, but you will eventually rely on that bond to keep you both calm when those bonds are tested by inevitable product failure. The more adept you become at bonding with human beings, the more influence you will have over the emotional situations that will arise.*

The Chameleon Mentality: Adapting to unchanging circumstances

An allegory relating to the dichotomy of personality types, this theory discusses the nature of adapting your own personality to the needs of others. In this world of unending differences in personalities, there are still only two personality types: trees and lizards. I chuckled when the thought first occurred to me, but as I began to examine this idea in my own workplace, more and more truth was discovered. Let us look at the two objects. First, the tree. What do we know about the tree? In looking at it, we find it is an entirely immovable object with roots planted deeply into the soil. We also can note the color of the leaves. There are many different types of trees, from the weeping willow to solid oak, yet they share the quality of immovability. Trees represent people, both customers and colleagues, who are set in their ways and object to change. "I have been here for a long time, and there is no reason to change" would be their mantra. One fine example is a guest who has had a plan set for six months to celebrate an anniversary and is therefore visiting with an unchanging purpose. Another case would be a person who is calling you because they have a flat tire. In either case, nothing on planet earth can change why they are there. The customers quite simply, are. To succeed in customer service, you must first embrace both the presence and permanence of the object. Countless times, I have heard complaints from team members who bemoan special requests and certain particulars about paying customers. Already, they have failed because they are not embracing that their customers "are". In earlier days of working in hospitality, I was oft mystified at the persistent and sometimes petulant ways of people. It wasn't until I truly embraced the permanence and presence of all my guests and welcomed the idea of a fully unpredictable habitat. With that mindset, the most unpredictable service environment was now fully predictable because I acknowledged the people and the pitfalls of my natural work environment. I knew my success had less to do with the hazards that will inevitably appear and more to do with how well I could emotionally navigate through the forest. Do you ever notice people doing more work just to avoid certain types of duties? Showing up to a job with fingers crossed hoping to "not have to deal" with something is certainly not the way to exist! That is what trees do. They are static, unchanging, and cannot adapt to an undulating landscape. To keep this in context, trees also have redemptive qualities like stability. Lizards need the trees! After all, trees convert carbon dioxide into oxygen, a necessity for all living beings on earth. They also provide shelter and comfort for a great many creatures. That stated we must objectively recognize the facts about trees. They are immovable and necessary, and there are neither good nor bad qualities but rather simple facts about them that we must acknowledge and welcome. Now, let us consider the lizard. Lizards are much smaller than trees and also rely on them for sustenance in the form of ants and other crawlies that they find particularly delectable. Most importantly, the best trait of a lizard is the ability to change color. Lizards move from tree to tree, shifting shades for success and survival in order to live to see tomorrow. There are birds of prey, dangerous weather patterns, and other random hazards for the lizard to consider, so the more successfully it can navigate through the woods the better off it will be.

For context, let us look at the customer or more specifically the hotel guest. These are certainly trees. The guest has a purpose of coming to your place of business and there can be a thousand reasons; wedding, celebration, business, family gathering, pleasure, etc. Naturally, you are gathering that we, the customer service professionals, are the lizards. As lizards, navigating from one guest to another as if we are jumping from tree to tree, we must discover the purpose of each tree to learn what it is and why it is there. Once those details are discovered, we must adapt.

Now, we all have a distinct personality. I tend to enjoy long conversations with guests and delivering highly personalized service. However, that is not necessarily the right shade of kelly green for every guest that I meet. A business traveler doesn't want to hear my life story and certainly lacks the time to share their own. Upon discovering the purpose of people, it is then that we use our instinct to change color at the right time. Having lived in the forest of hospitality for fifteen years, I continue to develop my ability to change shades in order to operate in the most symbiotic manner with my guests and clients. Each tree has a different manner in which it bends in the daily breezes of life, just as guests have different ways of reacting when the winds of change arrive and problems occur. In the end, it is how you shift your body posture, voice, eye contact and choice of words that will dictate your success in such a dynamic environment. Your success in this facet of life is entirely in your hands! Sometimes it is easy to feel powerless as a customer service professional. It took me some time to embrace the mandate of the business and to focus on my ability to adapt instead of attempting to force an immovable object to shift positions. You will find this applies to interoffice relationships as well. Some of your colleagues will never change and some will share your ability to adapt. It is up to you to identify and separate the trees from the lizards, so you can more effectively navigate through your own forest. For the trees in your life, here are some things to consider. How do they like to be communicated to? What do they personally find toxic in the workplace? What brings them the most sunshine? Focus on adapting to support their strengths instead of trying to force change that will likely never come. You don't have to change the way you do everything, but subtle changes based on their unchanging needs can go a long way to ensuring a long productive life in the forest.

Summary: *This is surely one of the more abstract theories because there are so many variables. However, take a moment and think of the deepest rooted trees you face on a daily basis. How can you more successfully work in a symbiotic way? How can you shift your colors? Are you a tree in some ways? How can you apply the chameleon mentality to help* *produce more fruit in your environment?*

Layered Service: Creating experiences worth remembering

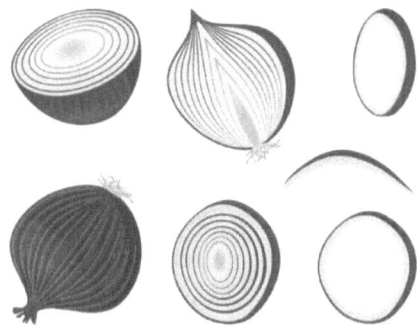

Onions, a staple of fabulous recipes from all regions of the world and simultaneously the reason restaurants present mints *along* with the check, are also a symbol of great service. Much like the onion, service should be spherical in nature, a three dimensional object with volume, mass, and weight - something a person can hold onto long after the experience has passed. Great service is something that can be remembered and will create an emotional connection, but it will not happen circumstantially. Service is a process and it functions very much like carefully peeling back the layers of an onion. A regular transaction goes as follows: A guest calls down to report a problem with their room, say, a lightbulb is burned out. The agent responds and states that they will send someone up right away. Agent then asks if they can help with anything else. Guest ends the call.

Now, at first glance it appears that the agent did the correct thing. They are taking care of the guest request, right? While the agent did the right *thing*, they failed to do it the right *way*. This is where layering service is very important. The service discussed previously is only two dimensional, a woeful question and answer session at best. Layer number one deals solely with the surface issue which, in this case, is an exhausted light bulb. Properly layering in another service requires the agent to take the initiative to ask a question unrelated to the original question, hence going a level deeper into the guest experience. If the original call was to correct an issue, a great follow up is "Is everything else working correctly in your room?" or "Is the rest of your accommodation to your liking?" Other easy questions like "What brings you here?" Or "How many nights will you be with us?" or "Do you have plans this evening?" can also be appropriate at times. People exhibit a tremendous response when asked a question about themselves in a customer service setting. After all, the self is often humanity's preferred subject of conversation. These types of simple questions will yield significant results.

First and most importantly, the guest is no longer focused on the issue at hand. A layered question makes for an easy detour off of Frustration Highway 101, a bumpy gravel road that nobody in the guest service industry prefers to drive on, mainly due to the number of casualties. What was a negative emotional connection is now transformed into something positive. It is the one extra hydrogen atom that turns a hydroxide ion into water. The guest will likely feel that the agent cares about their stay, and now there is a new opportunity for a service to be provided. If the guest has no plans, a dining reservation is recommended, or if the purpose of the visit is for a conference, directions to the guest's morning meeting and a wake-up call can be arranged. The number one priority for luxury hotels is to provide service, so to create a service opportunity out of thin air can only be considered time well spent. So often, what could be an exponentially beneficial moment for both the business and the guest only ends up a two dimensional and unremarkable experience. There is also a certain liberty about getting information from an individual with the sole purpose of funneling a new level of service in order to drive business goals.

Delving deeper into individual organizations, the art of customer service is a technique that needs to be taught in the training process, right along with the transactional side of service processes. Imagine how many individuals will feel empowered by being able to go deeper into the guest experience and understand that they have a new tool to use. How many undisclosed service issues will be uncovered? How much will customer satisfaction scores improve? So often individuals are trained solely on the transaction and not in the service art form. They are forced to learn the hard way, which can lead to a higher turnover and customer service scores will be static at best. It is like a teacher giving a final exam and only teaching half the material. To put it simply - it is unfair. It is up to organizations to incorporate a service layering methodology in their training, and great results will surely follow. It is time to add onions into your daily regimen. Just be sure to grab some mints for the breath of fresh air in your operation.

Summary: *Don't settle for the status quo. Find ways to develop dimensions in your one to one conversations with clients and customers. Give more than yes and no answers, and dig deeper into the customer experience. It is the only way you will find ways to improve their experience, which will ultimately improve yours.*

Lost in Translation: Speaking the right service language

In the blizzard of the average business day, people find themselves wearily ambling forward with frostbitten cheeks and without gloves. Things move fast. People move faster. At times they forget that while the snow is spinning in a seemingly random frenzy, each snowflake is unique in its design and purpose. Customer service, more specifically hotel guest service, is highly similar to the aforementioned scenario. Mother Nature provides two ingredients for blizzard like conditions; wind and snow. From a business and service perspective, it is vitally important to separate and differentiate the two. The wind represents the dynamic movement of the day; meetings, issuing discipline, and operational irregularities. These elements often impose challenges to completing the daily "checklist" items that must be done to ensure financial integrity and productivity. The snow represents the individuals who need to be serviced in order for the checklist to maintain any sense of viability. Without customers, there is no checklist simply because there is no business to maintain. Leaders must first ensure that their front line agents are prepared for the conditions present on that day, therefore the pre-shift briefing is of the utmost importance. Not only does it equip the team with the "hat and gloves" forecast of the day, but it also allows leaders to assess the preparedness of their front line workers. It is easy to tell if someone is distracted, disinterested, or in some unfortunate cases disassociated with the team. Once prepared for the day's conditions, they are now ready to step out into the open and be exposed to the elements of the day. At this point, this is where the game begins. There is a tendency among front line customer service agents to have a fairly universal approach, and it is an incredibly reactive one at best. They often allow the person on the other side of the counter to dictate the direction of the service process, when it should be the other way around. It becomes a classic case of someone who is taking their dog for a walk - who is really walking who? If the dog sees a squirrel dart across the street, it is easy to tell who is in control, and most of the time it isn't the person desperately holding onto their shorts as Rover scrambles over to the acorn tree.

The reason service processes fail, especially in person to person contact scenarios, is because the agent is speaking the wrong service language. People who travel are traveling for one of three reasons; business, conventions, and leisure. That is it. Suppose the agent were to inquire as to what has brought the guest to the hotel. Wouldn't that help clue them in as to what information would be helpful to that particular guest?

Indeed, strategic analysis of each guest is asking a lot of front line agents considering that they are handling so many interactions. With that in mind, the following is a service structure that I started using back when I was a Front Office Agent, and I have used it ever since in my day to day handling of people. By addressing the guest with three easy questions (not all at once of course), it will enable the agent to speak the right service language because they have a fundamental understanding of the guest's purpose for their visit. This theory creates a sense of intuitive service because, by understanding "why" the guest is present, we can make recommendations off of the information that is discovered. Guests are surprisingly open, to a fault at times, once they perceive that the person offering service is interested in them. If we understand what a guest is looking to accomplish from the initial arrival stage, the agent then knows how to direct and "walk" them to the fulfillment of their vision. So often we try to meet "guest satisfaction" goals on comment cards and surveys, but very seldom do we ask the right questions during the course of business in order to know what the customer's goals actually are. It is as if we are trying to hit the bulls-eye on an invisible target. The structure goes as such: After the initial greeting and at the outset of the arrival process the following questions need to be asked.

How are you? (Present) - This will give the agent an idea of how the guest is currently feeling on an emotional level. A typical response would be - "Well, I had long flight from New York and they lost my luggage, so it has been a little rough". Already, the agent has some insight as to the duration of the guests travel experience. This would set up for the agent to say "I have some complimentary items, such as a toothbrush, toothpaste, and a shaving kit. I will get them for you". The guest doesn't even have to ask.

What brings you to _____? (Past) - This will tap into the history of what brought the guest to the hotel - family reunion, wedding, convention, etc. At that point, the agent understands why the guest is there, so they can make recommendations, give directions to the chapel, meeting event, or particular spot where they may have arrangements already.

Do you have plans for this evening? (Future) - This question is the most fun because it is at the end of the conversation and it grants one last opportunity for the agent to seal the deal, so to speak. Hint: Remember that the last 10% of the conversation has 90% of the impact. The guest will feel very comfortable with the agent at that point, so they may ask a question that they weren't sure about asking. Also the agent can freewheel just a bit, so the guest feels at home.

The Present-Past-Future conversation structure really works, and it is a great tool to open and close guest encounters in a concise yet thorough way. It can also be used as a training tool for newer service agents who aren't as comfortable with opening and closing the first chapter of the guest's stay. Additionally, it establishes the agent as the one who is "walking the dog" and they can feel confident about leading the transaction from the very beginning. There is nothing like being confident as a front line agent, and this small tool can help in some really big ways. Most importantly, it helps the agent focus on the most important thing of all; each unique customer and keeps them from getting stranded in the blizzard.

Summary: *Discovering your customer is essential. If we fail to understand their purpose, we will fail to meet the goals of their visit. When you know where your guest is coming from, you can then speak the right language to ensure you connect. Taking that a step further, we can then intuitively act on the needs we discover in order to capture the heart of the customer and demonstrate the highest levels of hospitality.*

Gone Fishin': Reeling in Big Angry Fish

Customer service is like fishing. An odd concept to be sure, but through experiencing the uncertainty of daily events and the unpredictability quotient of human beings that the service industry entails, are in fact, similar to one of the oldest past times of humanity. First, the unpredictability quotient is as follows. The number of people you will handle throughout the day (P) plus the number of potential issues that can arise (I) raised to an exponent of how many circumstances your customer may have experienced up to a certain point in their day (x) divided by the number of hours worked during your day (H). The equation then is defined by $(P + I^x)/H$. Now for all you math whizzes, don't bother solving for the variables because the secret lies in the variable "x". "X" is and always will be infinite. The equation is an example of why customer service rookies and even some professionals become frustrated with their jobs. They simply fail to embrace the lack of predictability in their occupation. There is essentially a finite number of issues that may arise (this could be debated but for the sake of simplicity, there are truly only so many things that can go wrong with a burger, hotel room, or motor vehicle – with many issues being repetitive). There are also a finite number of people a representative will handle through the course of their day. Likewise, there are also a set number of hours to be worked in a business day. That leaves the variable "x" – the number of combinations of things that have contributed to the mood of your customer. It could be an issue with their air conditioner at home or perhaps their long wait at the gas station once they got into town. Maybe they have to put down an animal in the coming week or perhaps a moody teenager washed a red shirt with the whites and now the clothes are all pink. Aren't these all things that could frustrate, sadden or disappoint anybody? The unpredictability quotient demonstrates the chain reaction of unpredictable events of which the receiving service agent will have a collective total of zero knowledge or control.

Isn't this supposed to be like fishing? Indeed it is. Unpredictable animal behavior also has a heavy hand in fishing, as you cannot be certain what exactly is happening beneath the surface of the water. However, as you wait, feel and watch, the probability that you catch *something* increases and eventually happens! The same goes for customer service. The longer you stand behind that counter and handle business, the probability that something goes awry increases to the point of inevitability – and then it happens. The fish furiously strikes the dangling bait just like the guest rushes to the counter and begins to vocalize, in no uncertain terms, the wrong that has been done. Sounds like a relatively damning occupation, right? Not true! It is the fact that the person waiting to assist is not prepared when they should have been ready all along.

They weren't watching. They weren't waiting. Now they have a situation that is spiraling out of control. I realized this early on as a Concierge at a luxury hotel. I found myself continually frustrated when issues, that were neither my fault nor in my small realm of control, would combust right in my lap. A taxi tour failed to be booked, a table was unreserved or champagne was delivered to the wrong room. That stated, sometimes it was my fault! However, when you send someone a dinner confirmation on Tuesday for a dinner on Friday but forgot to book it, you certainly do not expect that angry call from the guest asking why he is at the restaurant at 7:30pm with no table reserved on Valentine's Day. It was then that I realized that it would never stop and the more I prepared myself to catch that fish – or handle that angry guest as it were – the more adept I would become. I finally embraced unpredictability.

So how do you get the fish into your boat? First, it is an exercise in patience. As a novice, the first reaction to a fish striking your line is to immediately reel it in. Enter Rule Number One and the most important principle of the Gone Fishin' Theory: **Let the Line Out**. Imagine you have an issue at any place of business and you try to vocalize it, only to be cut off with a curt apology. It is upsetting when the person across the counter begins to apologize for an issue they have not even heard in its entirety! This truly takes a conscious and focused emotional effort on the part of the employee. Most people are afraid that by letting a customer vocalize their frustration, they are thereby allowing the situation to spiral out of control. This is not the case! By letting out the line, you are accomplishing a great deal. First, you have emotionally removed yourself from the situation and will not take it personally, as you have remained the one in control. Secondly, this strategic approach allows you to be more objective and collect the facts without panicking or blurting out a vapid apology. Take this time to focus on what the customer is saying, as this is the ammunition for an effective apology. Letting the line out will prompt the offended individual to state – and re-state – their beliefs about the situation. For example: The customer states, in so many words, that **"X happened, and now Y is going on and now Z is going to**

happen." That typically would be the first burst of angst out of the guest and depending on the nature of the complaint and relative complexity, they will likely restate their assessment another time or two. For example, if it is a case of coffee not showing up when ordered, the person will have some sense of rationale in their mind. However, if they just checked in to their honeymoon suite and they found the remainder of a Cobb salad in one of the dresser drawers (yes, this has actually happened), they will be slightly more distressed. Regardless of the perceived severity of the matter, maintain eye contact, and use your nonverbal communication to express your interest. Therefore, after letting the line out apply Rule Number Two: **Obtain the Cause, Effect, and Result**. As touched upon earlier, there are a finite number of issues that can occur. It is critical to identify the difference between an issue and a situation. For example, the hotel has no hot water (**issue**). Mrs. Johnson has no hot water. She is a keynote speaker for the ACME Company and needs to get to the auditorium early to prepare herself (**situation**). Rule Number Three: **Use the Cause, Effect, and Result in the form of an apology**. This is truly the only way to demonstrate your ability to listen. To properly empathize with the guest, it is important to apologize for the full situation and not just the issue, essentially restating the original complaint back to the customer. **"Mrs. Johnson, I am sorry that X happened which affected Y and now you are rightly concerned about Z."** Naturally, you need to use some inflection in your voice and fluff the verbiage to sell your apology. Your only objective at this point is to earn trust. Once you are trusted the fish no longer swims away out of fear, and you can begin to reel it in with a solution. If the person on the other side of the counter doesn't trust you, they won't accept anything you have to offer. Now Rule Number Four: **Give options**. This rule took me awhile to figure out. When I first started crafting solutions for guests, I would begin to think about solutions for the guest as they were digressing about the matter and explaining their various dilemmas. However, I found that no matter how clever or ingenious the suggestion was the guest would still feel sorely inconvenienced and maintain a relatively high level of frustration. After telling the guest what I could do for them I would often hear "But that doesn't work for me…." Or "Is that the only option?" It was at that moment that Rule Number Four became apparent. The guest begins to feel more in control of the **situation** when they can choose. It is almost like those "choose your own adventure" books. It was a rather novel concept. Why not give the guest the full array of choices, so they are now part of the solution by being empowered to make a decision regarding an **issue** that is completely out of their control? Look at the issue with no water, there are many potential solutions. The most straightforward fix is to suggest having a maintenance employee take a look at the matter. However, there may be a more severe problem that will be unable to be rectified, so perhaps changing rooms is an option. Suppose the guest has already been in their room for a couple days and moving would be a major inconvenience. Perhaps offering a shower at the spa facility is an option. This method allows full customization to truly and accurately accommodate the guest according to their preferences and needs. "Mrs. Johnson, I understand that you need to get to your meeting right away and our current water situation is far from ideal. I do have options for you and will help in any way that I can."

Let us recap the rules:

Rule Number 1: Let the line out. Give the guest the time to express their feelings and explain their unique situation.

Rule Number 2: Obtain the Cause, Effect, and Result. As the person expresses the details, listen for what happened, who it happened to, and the expected outcome for the individual.

Rule Number 3: Use the information from Rule Number 2 in the form of an apology. "I am sorry that X happened to Y and now you are in this Z circumstance."

Rule Number 4: Give at least two options to the person who was inconvenienced. Knowing the details of their unique situation will help you decide which options to present depending on how urgently they need a solution.

If you can successfully proceed through the first four rules, you can now safely land the fish in your boat with **Rule Number 5: Follow up**. People can sense fear, and it can certainly be a fear inducing experience when you receive unexpected hostility from a complete stranger. Nothing says you are unafraid like a personal follow up. In some instances, the guest may actually apologize to you for how they acted! It is a real clincher when you ensure that the resolution you helped facilitate was satisfactory – or hopefully better than expected. Most guests and customers expect employees in the service industry to avoid them if they had an unpleasant encounter. By showing you are a true professional with a solid follow up, they will admire your courage and chances are pretty good that you will have built a relationship through the adversity that you both experienced. It is quite a bond to be sure, and I have made some lifelong friends through strange things that have happened.

Here is a specific situation that actually occurred. We had a major water outage of roughly fifteen hundred rooms in a busy Las Vegas hotel filled with convention attendees. What did that mean? Essentially, most were on the schedule of waking up at 7:00am to make the convention at 8:00am only to return around 5:00pm to shower at 6:00pm and head to a function at 7:00pm. At least half the hotel had people showering at the same time. You can imagine the flood (no pun intended) of complaints that occurred in the morning and late afternoon. This was truly an exercise in effective apologizing. It was important to listen to each complaint and understand the full situation and not just the issue that was occurring. There was one issue but a plethora of situations. For one guest it was not being able to adequately prepare notes for a speaking engagement but for another it was they were now running late for a 50th anniversary dinner for their parents. Enter Mrs. Johnson. I had been handling guests for about an hour and was resolving things as best I could, when I saw a flash of shiny black flats and tightly pulled back brunette hair atop an excessively pale canvas glide across the floor like an albino cobra dressed up for the senior prom. I had just finished up with a family of five people who were attempting to shower after coming back from the pool. I worked out something with the hotel that connected to ours, so at the very least they were situated and could take a proper shower. I had just wiped the gooey remains of the sand and red lollipop mixture off the granite counter when Mrs. Johnson seemingly teleported herself to the desk. Fortunately for me, she wasn't carrying a broom as far as I could tell so my initial fear of being spontaneously turned into a newt quickly dissipated. She was one of those guests who had gotten herself just beyond boiling while waiting for the elevator to get her down off the 60th floor. My good evening was disregarded as she began to unfurl her tale of woe. Naturally, seeing what was now a line of at least three more individuals behind her – one in a suit and the other two in beach wear – I knew they were likely suffering from the same water issue. I also knew I would have to dig deep on the one in front of me. Mrs. Johnson began to relay the events of her day. It started with a missed wake-up call and an errant breakfast order – she had asked for her eggs to be scrambled and not over-easy. She barely made it to her meeting where they had an audio-visual malfunction which compromised the lunch hour. She was now in danger of not being able to properly prep her keynote speech because she was unable to take a proper shower.

First, I obeyed **Rule One** and **let the line out**. I let her get the whole story out. Now I didn't just stand there and stare. I had my notepad, and occasionally glanced down to write but immediately looked back up and gave affirmative nods. I used words like "understood" and "indeed", just general affirmative and timed responses. I don't like saying "I understand". How can I truly understand if I haven't heard the whole story? As she began to conclude, I set down my pen and kept my hands on the desk. Clearly she was done and I could sense the initial wave of anger was over. I then employed the action from **Rule Two** and had obtained the **Cause, Effect and Result**. I then used that information in the form of an **Apology** (**Rule Three**). I said, "Mrs. Johnson, this is definitely not how your day was supposed to go. You had several items go awry this morning only to see you visit your room to get ready with no hot water. I know you need to prepare your notes for your keynote speech as soon as possible. I do have options for you and we can get moving in the right direction." Next I used **Rule Four, Give Options**. I let her know she could utilize the Spa and I could assist with her items but I also let her know that I had a vacant room on another floor if she wished to use that room in conjunction with her current accommodation. She opted for the second option as she didn't feel comfortable getting ready in a semi-private area. Since she obviously was sensitive to privacy, I sent one of my female team members to assist her with shifting a few items to the new room. Lastly, I employed **Rule Five**, **Follow Up**. While she was at her event, we had a card and flowers sent to the room. We customized the card with her company logo and the whole team at the Front Desk signed the card with warm wishes. I made a point to visit her at breakfast the following morning just to ensure that she was finally situated. She was very surprised that I would seek her out after she berated me in public. I chuckled and let her know that the most important thing was that she needed to conquer her very important moment and that all other sentiments and words were simply circumstantial.

When it comes to resolving situations big or small, remember that it is always big for the customer. If it really didn't matter, they wouldn't bring it up. That is why you should treat them all with the same sincerity. Remember the Sylvester Stallone Theory. It isn't up to us to decide what is valid, invalid, major, minor, or medium. We are here to do and if we do, we might as well do it at the highest level possible. Personally, I refuse to pick and choose when and where I attain the most positive results. Life is like a treasure hunt, and to leave one stone unturned is to leave one gold coin unfound. You have the power to maximize the positivity in each interaction with people, no matter what side of the counter you are on. Our power to influence emotion and decision making runs deep, but it is a matter of how much effort we put into each encounter.

Remember, this problem solving outline is merely a template to build on. You will find ways to add to and alter it, but by following these five principles you have a model for success!

Summary: *Embracing the fact that you are fishing is a very big step. Come to work ready for problems! Don't live in fear, but simply be prepared. Study the five rules and practice. There is a bit of a rhythm to the process, but if you practice the steps, you can truly become a master. Trust the system – it works if you do!*

3D Service: The Ultimate Experience

How do you take a movie and make it look better, sound clearer, and make it even more real? Shoot it in 3D! It is truly amazing what they are doing with digital cinema these days, and I personally love seeing my favorite films in 3D. After all, I have worn corrective lenses since the first grade so the glasses are a natural look anyway. Many people are curious how to make personalized service really pop, and there is actually a simple, three step method. It is truly as simple as three "D"s!

Discover

As discussed in earlier segments of this book, discovery is an essential element in making people feel good. If you ask a relevant question to someone, you are very likely to get a fairly detailed response. Simply discovering people is an art form by itself. For example, when I go to the grocery store, I have a particular question for the person behind the register. My objective is to simply personalize the transaction and then take it slightly beyond what many would consider to be a "normal" transaction. This inclines the individual to perform better because they are now accountable for their actions in what will be a more memorable encounter. I like to inquire "are you at the beginning, middle, or end of your shift?" This triggers the response and there is no wrong answer, because I have a fun little nugget to share regardless of their reply. If the person says "beginning", I simply encourage them to stay focused and remind them to have a healthy snack. If they say "middle", I say "Wow, already over the hump! Nice!" If they say "end", I say "Look at that, you will be off in no time at all!" All I did was discover something about the person and take just a moment to act on it in a positive way. I don't have to ask that particular question, but if I want to practice the art of moving people in an emotionally positive trajectory, it is an easy way to start. It is simply a case of emotional inertia – what is in motion tends to stay in motion. If the direction is positive, there is a high probability of continuing that motion. Remember, discovering facts and details about your customers is only valuable when you choose to act on it. Give it a try at your local grocery store or any place of business and watch what happens. Once you get comfortable with that, begin using your favorite tagline question on your customers. They will open up and you will begin to take the first step to multi-dimensional service. Like all things, practice makes perfect. Monitor the body language and demeanor of your customers and begin to note the difference in the way they act around you.

Direct

Now that we have discovered something about our customer, we are now in a position to direct them. Suppose there is a family of four checking into a hotel in Las Vegas on a sizzling summer day. Dad is wearing his Red Sox cap and the son and daughter have their baseball gloves attached to their backpacks. You make the discovery – "How was your trip in from the Northeast?" Come to find out they are actually on a road trip and they have stopped in Illinois, Wyoming, and Colorado. In those formative moments, there is a litany of information on these folks. They have been traveling for days, enjoy baseball, the kids are the same age, and they have never been this far west. With plenty of information to act on, your next move must to be spontaneous and unexpected. The spa is recommended for Mom and Dad, the new baseball exhibit down The Strip would be great for the whole gang, and there is a restaurant next to the exhibit that is perfect for families. Without the discovery element, none of that would be possible! Immediately the family is engaged and you have exponentially elevated your personal value! Several things could arise: increased hotel revenue via Spa and restaurant, potential gratuity for you, and reduced probability of getting yelled at. You may laugh when reading that last phrase, but this is where your power truly exists. By spending the time bonding with this family in that moment, you have formulated a relationship and relationships are built in order to withstand inevitable adversity.

Divulge

Now that the guest is comfortable with you, the customer service agent, a different dynamic exists. You made a small investment in them that will pay off in a big way. Suppose those guests whom you have just wowed with your Discovery and Direction get up to their room and it just doesn't have the view they are looking for. Perhaps there is actually something wrong inside. One time I checked in a hotel guest and they found a Cobb salad in their dresser drawer! They came back to the desk nonplussed but because we had an emotionally meaningful check in together, they treated me like a human being and I was able to more efficiently resolve the matter. Instead of just dealing with it problems that arise, customers will feel comfortable bringing irregularities up to you personally. They can count on you to help, because after all, you have been so helpful from the start. Also, due to the bond you share and no matter how small it may seem, the customer will react in a more positive way when adversity arises. I have seen too many situations that could have been avoided if only the customer service agent had managed the guest's emotions from the start. Most of the reason customers get angry is because they believe that being vocal is simply the only way to get you to care about them. If you educate them that you care from the very beginning, via Discovery and Direction, you will have fewer worries about the Jekyll & Hyde guest catching you off guard. This strategy is about managing customer emotions before they become compromised. Isn't it easier to go from neutral to positive rather than negative to neutral? The secret is developing a deep sense of trust so customers will feel comfortable in quietly divulging things they may not normally share. Truth be told, most guests don't want to complain. As a customer service professional, think of how many transactions you actually perform per day and compare the good ones with the not so good ones. There is actually a huge disparity! It is the negative ten percent of encounters that poison ninety percent of our short term memory. Too often businesses recognize failure when it is too late. Once the customer has left the building, there is no longer any opportunity to recover.

Summary: *Discover, Direct, & the Guest will Divulge details that you need to know. Managing the* *emotions of the customer from the first moment is the key to your individual success. Don't wait for disaster to strike! Manage emotions while they are still manageable in order to maximize the benefit of happy customers. 3D Service is only as legendary as you make it!*

Theories in Action:

You will find below a series of recaps I used to send out at the end of my shift as a Guest Services Agent at a four diamond resort in the Caribbean. It gives a glimpse of some of the theories in action, and it also explains some of the hilarity that can ensue. All names and room numbers have been changed.

Pound it....Recap for 2/18/08

Greetings sports fans,

there was lots of action to be had today in GSR. Naturally my standard activities applied:

Comfort Checks -

Simmons: Mrs. had a GI virus from the cruise ship they just left. Mr. S was out playing tennis until noon. I asked her if she needed anything, but she already had tea. She did order a turkey sandwich on french bread/baguette with lettuce and tomato (no mayo or mustard) and she thought she might try some soup. Well, that led me back down to the front. I knew I needed to get this sandwich and soup in a timely manner. Since this wasn't an official menu item, I thought it best to see the whole sandwich process through, since, after all, it's only a turkey sandwich. Well, I went to Room Service first to let them know I had an order. I went to put it in directly at the bar. I was told they had no sliced turkey with which to make this sandwich, and that "if I went to get the turkey and brought it to the bar, then the sandwich could get made." So, instead of parading around the Front Office with a wad of turkey, I went to the Box Lunch Prep Center. There my sandwich was made. However, when Janet saw me in there waiting for the finishing touches on the sandwich, she decided to lay into me at a verifiably loud volume about the following points:

A. Why am I in the food prep station without a health card?
B. Why don't I just drop off the paper and let her handle it?
C. Don't let the bar tell me that they don't have any turkey (not sure where that one was going)

Naturally, I was not afforded an opportunity to

respond and break down the arguments posed against my actions. Needless to say, I brought the sandwich to room service (and the soup), and it was promptly delivered to room 501. I checked on Mrs. Simmons around 2pm (the order was delivered around 12:30pm....a half an hour turnaround after the order was taken, which isn't bad, but considering that I had to badger around to see that this was accomplished, I feel the time would have been longer sans badgering). Anyway, Mrs. Simmons was glad I checked back on her, and she needed a new Fire Alarm battery that was replaced shortly after I called it in.

I visited Mr. Frost launder at 10am. He was jovial.

The Golds went up to tea a little later than the usual time.

The Weilmans had a great time on their sail.

The Komans dropped the Kid's off at Kid's Club and had a great day.

Browns went on their fishing trip. I haven't gotten a success report.

Mr. Rowland is happy to be back and I got him his keys at 2:30pm.

I had a nice chat with Mr. Goodfriend.

I saw the Walsh party off on their 9:30am sail.

Lots of running around, but I maintained an efficient presence. It was pretty awesome to get the Romans back in house. Well, I am going to go running and prepare for Saturday. Have a good night.

Solo Hammering...recap for 3/21/08

With April Fool's day around the corner, today called for no nonsense. I finally shipped out Mr. Sterling's bags this morning, so it was nice to get that out of the way. Comfort checks took forever, as I spent some time at the Front Desk and concierge today. The time was well spent, and I encountered some guests that I originally would not have met. The notables were:

Glidden in 502 - Made Kid's Club/Babysitting arrangements. Had a nice chat.

Corland 809 - Had tons of questions about boat trips, itineraries and surrounding islands. Kind of intense.

I saw the Maclins a few times today (I roomed them yesterday). It was their first whole day, so they had questions about Cruz Bay and fun stuff. Once again, that encounter reinforced the importance of rooming. I like rooming as many people as possible, so when I go comfort checking, it's not like "Hey, I'm some strange dude who gets paid to check on you." It's more like

"Oh hey, Jeremy is here, let's ask him something." It sounds weird, but the whole dynamic of the conversation is changed by just that one early encounter during the stay. That type of comfort check is, for lack of a better word, more comfortable, and their chances of telling me about a small problem are increased as well. This business is more than just "faces in the window" and hunting to find problems. It is about caring for the people who essentially are staying in our home, many of whom live lives of heavy traffic, economic uncertainty, and high levels of stress, and this is our way of giving them back their freedom to be happy and allow them to do whatever they want. Okay, enough of the tangent.

Baxter 1170 - Set up Jeep Rental/dinner. They like the property

I saw Mr. Schaefer at the Buffet. He said that the resort is awesome. Very nice (Borat voice).

Catch of the Day:

Mrs. Fielding in room 703: The artist didn't show up for the lesson at 1:00pm (which I have a confirmation email sent on 3/23 from her regarding this lesson and its confirmation). Val called me at 1:15 to let me know that the artist wasn't there, so I raced up to The Patio to try to get them before they made it to the desk. Well, I missed them, so I just went back to the Front Desk and waited for them, since I knew that's where they would surely be headed. They were very unhappy about it, PLUS, it was a 40th anniversary gift from their son. She had also booked massages for 3:00pm tomorrow, which I confirmed right away, so they could be at ease. I also applied their Gift Card to their guest bill, per their request.

I roomed the Birds (1106), and the Colters (1201). Nice folks.
It was busy but thoroughly covered with little GSR footprints.

See you tomorrow.

Driving the nail home - Recap for 03/03/08

With the pick-up of a jolly old man at 10:15 (Haskins) approaching and a site experience at 11 pending, I knew I would be in for a fun day. I was hoping to annihilate a few comfort checks early, so I hit both breakfast outlets. I only got a couple in, but they were key (Pastor and Robbins) since I had roomed them the night before. Mr. Haskins harped on a few things after he got back from his taxi tour and a couple of things resonated with me: When his breakfast hamper was delivered, it was set on the floor, and it took both he and his wife to get it onto the table. They saw the tablecloth and silverware inside, but had to set the table themselves. It may not be standard practice, but due to their apparent age and ability (or lack thereof), a little assistance should be customarily offered. Their bags were set on the floor and not placed on the luggage rack. Once again, a lack of attentiveness to their present state. He was a professor at the University of Miami which I found very interesting. He is still a Hurricanes fan.

The site inspection went very well and I gave them the

full scope of the quintessential Resort experience. They were shown rooms 504 and 280 which had been made up to specifications.

Today's list of victims (guests who I had thorough informative conversations/inquiries with) is as follows: Robbins, Pastor, Roth, Stallman, Moyer, Grasslin, Haskins, Kinderland, Jones, Rasmussen, D'lavio, Elderman, McFurlan, Doran, Hassick, Gustaf)

Lots of randomness floated my way. It was as if I was a GIANT Blue Whale and all of these little plankton just floated into my waiting jaws....What a happy Blue Whale I was.....Here is my list of plankton:

1. Room 140 - I saw them pacing around the Taxi Stand and they were waiting for their bags. Bags were supposed to be up there at 10am but it was 10:20, so I had the FD call the bellman and they got them up there right away.

2. Mr. Harvey said the scent in 802 had returned when they cranked up the A/C. They left today, but just thought we should know.

3. Mr. Moore in 328 had sent a fax out a couple days ago and wanted it back in his room immediately. Rosa called me to see if I could track it down, which we did, and I delivered it with a handwritten note from myself to apologize for the latency and that if he needed anything further he could contact me directly (left my cell).
mmmmm.....more plankton.....
4. Ms. Jessie needed flat rate post office boxes.....hammered it.

5. Mr. Moyer had left some pictures in his seat on the airplane yesterday. I called Arna and SHE hammered it and got the pictures from the plane, and sent them on the 4pm boat. Meanwhile, Priscilla picked up some grapefruit soda, since apparently we were out (wtf????), and it all was subsequently delivered.

After that.....I was a very happy blue whale.....I hope the cocktail party was a blast and I will see you all Thursday.

Release the hounds!!....Recap for 1/8/08

Greetings fellow seekers of the hotel vision......

Ollie....you don't have to read all my jibber jabber if you don't want to. You can skip to the **bold** type about the birdfeeders.

Today, while short on the bag overhead, I was long on the guest contact which is the kind of day that I particularly enjoy. I had plenty of time to chat with my comfort checks, so I was able to dole out plenty of inside tips. Ms. Donald (room 1140 under the last name Cherry) had many questions about the resort and was interested in the yoga but was afraid it was too "weird". I told her that she should definitely consider one of the introductory classes like the Basic Yoga, and that she could decide then if she wanted to delve deeper into the world of yoga.

Mr. Winkleman in 103 was pumped about being

close to the beach, and since they got in late, they needed some orientating. One thing to note is that the guests are not being informed about breakfast and lunch on the west side of the property. I always make sure to push that to guests staying on the far beaches. I mention the beauty of the setting and the exclusivity of the location to resort guests only, and the guests really take to that information. I anticipate seeing more people there for the rest of the week (Cherry, Barnes. Winkleman, and Theodore will likely be up there a couple times). Guests know they are paying top dollar, so I always try to mention things that ONLY resort guests can do, so they feel privileged to be here.....which they are!!!! Westside breakfast and lunch have been extremely quiet, which means the main buffet is rocking (a good thing) but also compromising quality breakfast service (a bad thing). I met Theodore and Barnes after their Hot Yoga sessions this morning, so we had nice chats about hiking, dining, and resort history.

Mr. Stein was super happy about his massages.

Mrs. Kohl called me this AM asking for Priscilla, so I said that you (Priscilla........me Tarzan.....) could meet her tomorrow morning. Oh yeah, I set up an email notification alarm with Lotus, so we'll see if it works. Well, I wound up running into her as I was attempting to deliver a vehicle to the Wedding Planners, and we had a nice half hour chat. Here is the Cliff's Notes version:

1. The manager's cocktail party wasn't posted and they didn't know where it was

2. The movie was posted last night, but not shown

3. There aren't any bird feeders between the verandah and the dining room. She misses seeing the birds. Is there any way we can get a couple feeders, so she can be reunited with the Bananaquits?

4. Our fancy restaurant is closed too many nights.

Priscilla, you should definitely say hello to Mrs. Kohl at breakfast tomorrow morning, but I think most of her venting is out. I took her steam like a wool suit!

I thanked her for her comments because return guests voice their opinions since they care about the resort. I totally agreed and thanked her once again. She loved the new orchid arrangement in the garden area, so I ordered a $50.00 orchid arrangement from the flower shop to put in her room.

Priscilla, nice hook-up with the insect oil. They love it!!! (room 304)

We need to have a movie put on for Ms. Jessie and the Kohl's each night in the Activity Center. Something classic. I will have the concierge put one on tonight. Tomorrow, I can check the video store for another 60's or 70's Hollywood favorite.

That's all for now.

Guest Letters

5-8-11

Dear Jeremy,

Many, many thanks for facilitating all the arrangements these last five days.

You make a big difference for many people including us.

Cheers,
Bonnie & Les Max

Jan 30, 2011

Jeremy

    Thank you for the excellent hospitality we enjoyed during our stay. The kind attention of all of the staff was a pleasure.

    This will likely be our last travel adventure. Beth Ann's cancer challenges her more each day. We selected a great place to create a few more memories.

    Sincerely

    John

Thursday, March 10, 2011

Dear Jeremy

The "care and feeding" of my mom is a new journey for us.

Your assistance made our stay more comfortable and worry-free.

Thanks again for your thoughtfullness & hospitality

Good bye for now...
Betty, Judy & Po

Dear Jeremy,

It is true that a person who loves his job is a person who will always be good at it, as you are easily both.

Even the simplest questions, requests, or concerns are very important to you as you constantly juggle the diverse needs of those you see everyday.

Just knowing that you were there to help us with the small things allowed us the peace of mind to enjoy the larger parts of our trip to this beautiful island.

Please thank Laura, Melena, JT & Roma for their gracious

Closing

It is an incredible work that we do and often times it is a labor of love. I hope this book inspired new ideas and processes for the readers because our business requires innovation and new ways of thinking. It is only by documenting and expressing our thoughts and ideas that we can continue to grow. As technology continues to delicately weave itself between humans and their products, there will always exist a need for a human connection. The more effectively we can emotionally move our clients, guests, customers, and colleagues the greater our influence will be on the next generation of service requests.

In your service,

Jeremy

About The Author

Jeremy Zuber was raised in a small suburb of Des Moines, Iowa. Although travel means were rather modest while he was young, he always loved going new places and seeing new things. Originally, his plan was to spend one final collegiate summer in the mountains of Wyoming. When the dishwasher position was unavailable, he soon found himself employed as a Bellman at a historic, four diamond lodge. Eventually, he took a seasonal position at a resort in the Caribbean and spent his twenties working summers as a Bellman in the Grand Tetons and winters as a Concierge in the U.S. Virgin Islands. After a brief stint in Florida, he met a hotel guest named Michelle and married her. Life whisked them away to Las Vegas and then back to the Caribbean which has always felt like home. After fifteen years of work in hospitality, he has never been more enthused with the industry or more motivated by the future.

www.ingramcontent.com/pod-product-compliance
Lightning Source LLC
Chambersburg PA
CBHW030915180526
45163CB00004B/1843